EP Third Reader Workbook

Easy Peasy
All-in-One
Homeschool

I'm _____.

This is my workbook. My favorite books are

_____

_____

_____.

Contents

ACTIVITIES USING WORDS FROM DAY 45

ACTIVITIES USING WORDS FROM DAY 120

REVIEW ACTIVITIES USING ALL WORDS

BONUS ACTIVITIES

SOLUTIONS TO SELECTED PUZZLES

About this Workbook

This is an offline workbook of vocabulary puzzles and games for Easy Peasy All-in-One Homeschool's reading course for Level 3. We've modified and expanded upon the online activities available at the Easy Peasy All-in-One Homeschool website (www.allinonehomeschool.com) so that your child can work completely offline if desired. Whether you use the online or offline versions, or a combination of both, your child will enjoy these supplements to the Easy Peasy reading course.

How to use this Workbook

Although this workbook can be used as a stand-alone learning resource, or even just for fun, it is designed to be used in conjunction with Easy Peasy's reading curriculum, either the online or offline version. As you proceed through the EP reading course, use this workbook to practice the vocabulary words indicated.

This workbook follows the EP reading course systematically. As the table of contents clearly shows, all activities for the words from *Day X* of the EP reading course are grouped together. Pick out an activity under *Day X* and have your child work on it.

If your child initially has difficulty remembering all the words, don't worry. The first activity under *Day X* is always to review and read aloud all the words and their meanings. The matching activities provided are another a great way to reinforce the meanings of the words in preparation for the more challenging exercises in the workbook.

Aesop's Fables Vocabulary

Review and read aloud the words and their meanings.

quarrel	= to have an argument
fierce	= ferocious, wild and violent
reconcile	= become friends again
necessity	= something that is needed
contemptuous	= acting like someone else is beneath you
persuade	= to use words to convince someone of something

✓ The Dolphins <u>quarreled</u> with the Whales, and before very long they began fighting with one another. The battle was very <u>fierce</u> and had lasted some time without any sign of coming to an end, when a Sprat thought that perhaps he could stop it; so he stepped in and tried to <u>persuade</u> them to give up fighting and make friends. But one of the Dolphins said to him <u>contemptuously</u>. "We would rather go on fighting till we're all killed than be <u>reconciled</u> by a Sprat like you!"
   – *The Dolphins, the Whales, and the Sprat*
✓ <u>Necessity</u> is the mother of invention.
   - *The Crow and the Pitcher*

Aesop's Fables Matching

Can you match the words with their definitions?

"I thought those Grapes were ripe,
but I see now they are quite sour."
- *The Fox and the Grapes*

| quarrel | ● | ● | ferocious, wild and violent |

| fierce | ● | ● | something that is needed |

| reconcile | ● | ● | to have an argument |

| necessity | ● | ● | become friends again |

| persuade | ● | ● | acting like someone else is beneath you |

| contemptuous | ● | ● | to use words to convince someone of something |

Aesop's Fables Spelling

acting like someone else is beneath you

C			T			P	T				

something that is needed

N				S				Y

become friends again

R		C			C		

to use words to convince someone of something

P				U		D	

to have an argument

Q					E	

ferocious, wild and violent

F			R		

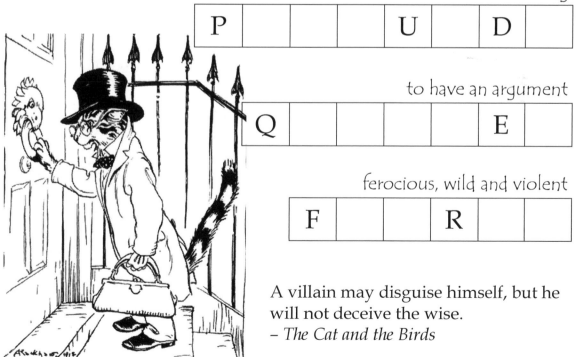

A villain may disguise himself, but he
will not deceive the wise.
– *The Cat and the Birds*

11

Aesop's Fables Crossword

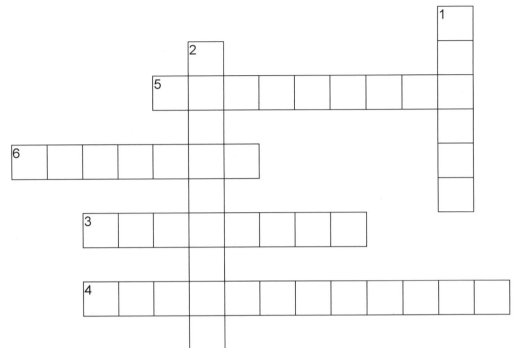

Across

3. to use words to convince someone of something
4. acting like someone else is beneath you
5. become friends again
6. to have an argument

Down

1. ferocious, wild and violent
2. something that is needed

The Fox and the Stork

Aesop's Fables Word Pieces

Use the pieces below to build words with the given definitions.

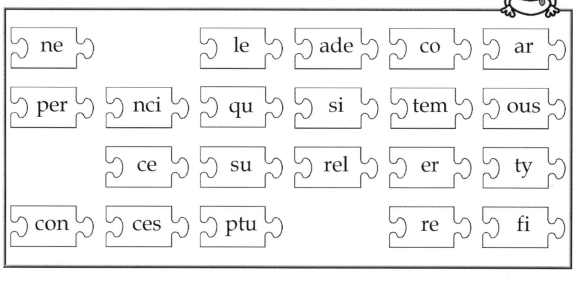

ne le ade co ar

per nci qu si tem ous

ce su rel er ty

con ces ptu re fi

to have an argument

ferocious, wild and violent

become friends again

something that is needed

to use words to convince someone of something

acting like someone else is beneath you

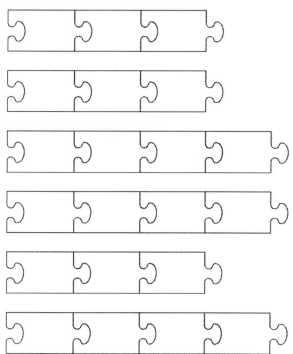

13

Aesop's Fables Fill-in-the-Blanks

Fill in the blanks to complete the sentences. Change the word forms if necessary.

quarrel	RECONCILE	necessity
contemptuous	fierce	persuade

1. The Dolphins _____ with the Whales, and before very long they began fighting with one another. The battle was very _____, and had lasted some time without any sign of coming to an end, when a Sprat thought that perhaps he could stop it; so he stepped in and tried to _____ them to give up fighting and make friends. But one of the Dolphins said to him _____, "We would rather go on fighting till we're all killed than be _____ by a Sprat like you!"
   - *The Dolphins, the Whales, and the Sprat*

2. _____ is the mother of invention.
   - *The Crow and the Pitcher*

14

Heidi I Vocabulary

Review and read aloud the words and their meanings.

enmity	=	hatred
scold	=	reproach
vigorous	=	strong and active
vexed	=	frustrated and annoyed
luscious	=	highly pleasing to the senses
imposing	=	grand and impressive in appearance
acquaintance	=	a person you know but not very well
loiter	=	to dawdle over your work or to hang around some place without any purpose

- ✓ I'm rather <u>vexed</u> with him. He never puts the tools away.
- ✓ If you <u>scold</u> your child too much, he will lose confidence.
- ✓ The United States is a young, <u>vigorous</u> country.
- ✓ They fight because there is <u>enmity</u> between them.
- ✓ Teenagers were <u>loitering</u> in the street outside.
- ✓ An <u>imposing</u> house towers high over the hill.
- ✓ He is not a friend, only an <u>acquaintance</u>.
- ✓ The herb garden is full of <u>luscious</u> herbs.

Heidi I Matching

Can you match the words with their definitions?

vexed   luscious

enmity   scold

imposing   loiter

acquaintance   vigorous

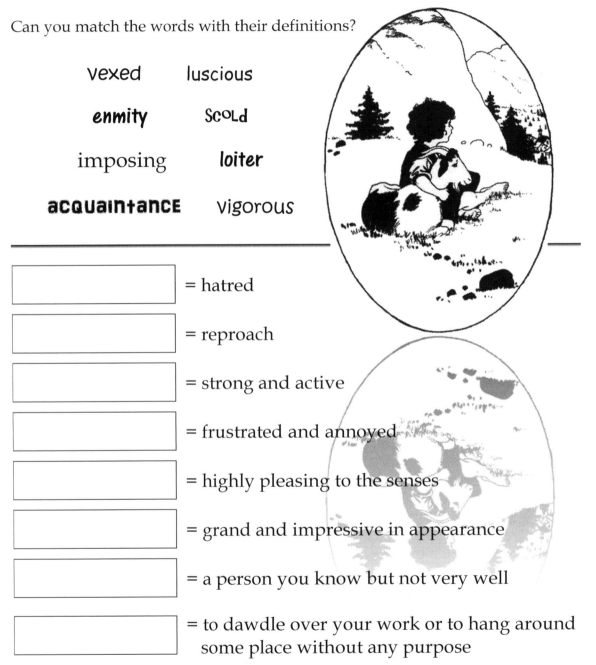

☐	= hatred
☐	= reproach
☐	= strong and active
☐	= frustrated and annoyed
☐	= highly pleasing to the senses
☐	= grand and impressive in appearance
☐	= a person you know but not very well
☐	= to dawdle over your work or to hang around some place without any purpose

Heidi I Spelling

a person you know but not very well

A		Q				T			

grand and impressive in appearance

I		P	O			

highly pleasing to the senses

L		C				S

frustrated and annoyed

V		X		

reproach

S				D

hatred

E			I		

strong and action

V		G			U	

Heidi I Word Jumble

Unscramble the jumbled words.

strong and active

ORUSOIVG → _____

a person you know but not very well

NCATAENQUIAC → _____

frustrated and annoyed

EXEVD → _____

grand and impressive in appearance

POMGNSII → _____

highly pleasing to the senses

CSOUUILS → _____

reproach

OCLSD → _____

hatred

EMNYIT → _____

to dawdle over your work or to hang around without purpose

LIRETO → _____

Heidi I Word Search

Find the hidden words and explain their meanings. The words can go in any direction, even backwards! The solution is on page 71.

A	W	M	X	S	L	O	I	T	E	R	A	U	V
S	O	K	H	R	U	V	U	N	D	C	Q	G	E
P	M	D	L	C	J	O	G	X	Q	Y	Y	N	X
F	Z	P	U	V	N	R	I	U	B	T	T	I	E
A	N	L	K	E	Y	P	A	C	I	A	C	S	D
S	U	O	R	O	G	I	V	M	S	W	R	O	P
S	M	Q	M	V	N	O	N	Y	Q	U	M	P	Z
U	C	A	S	T	I	E	H	J	C	Z	L	M	O
N	P	O	A	Y	P	O	G	R	S	Q	O	I	T
Q	P	N	L	T	I	N	B	Y	U	E	T	U	D
X	C	W	P	D	N	S	F	P	Q	R	N	X	B
E	T	A	S	R	R	O	V	X	M	W	E	O	V

enmity   luscious

loiter   vigorous

imposing   vexed

acquaintance   scold

19

Heidi I Fill-in-the-Blanks

Fill in the blanks to complete the sentences. Change the word forms if necessary.

imposing	VEXED	loiter	vigorous
SCOLD	luscious	enmity	acquaintance

1. I'm rather _____ with him. He never puts the tools away.

2. If you _____ your child too much, he will lose confidence.

3. The United States is a young, _____ country.

4. They fight because there is _____ between them.

5. Teenagers were _____ in the street outside.

6. An _____ house towers high over the hill.

7. He is not a friend, only an _____.

8. The herb garden is full of _____ herbs.

Heidi II Vocabulary

Review and read aloud the words and their meanings.

evade =	to avoid
console =	to comfort
compensation =	a payment for something
despondent =	feeling gloomy or discouraged
obtrusive =	butting in, intruding on another's space
pungent =	something with a really strong taste or smell
earnest =	serious about what you mean or what you're doing
piteous =	used to describe something that you feel sorry for
indignation =	righteous anger, feeling upset by something that is unjust or not right
contempt =	a feeling of despising toward people who are dishonorable or beneath you

- ✓ It was a <u>piteous</u> sight to see.
- ✓ He is <u>earnest</u> in his endeavors.
- ✓ She looked at him with <u>contempt</u>.
- ✓ The taste is similar, but not as <u>pungent</u>.
- ✓ You always laugh and <u>evade</u> the question.
- ✓ She earns a lot of <u>compensation</u> for her work.
- ✓ Nothing could <u>console</u> him when his wife died.
- ✓ When I was robbed, I was filled with <u>indignation</u>.
- ✓ It's difficult to work with a loud, <u>obtrusive</u> person.
- ✓ My little brother was <u>despondent</u> after losing the game.

21

Heidi II Matching

Can you match the words with their definitions?

> console   pungent   **compensation**   evade   obtrusive
> piteous   contempt   **DESPONDENT**   indignation   earnest

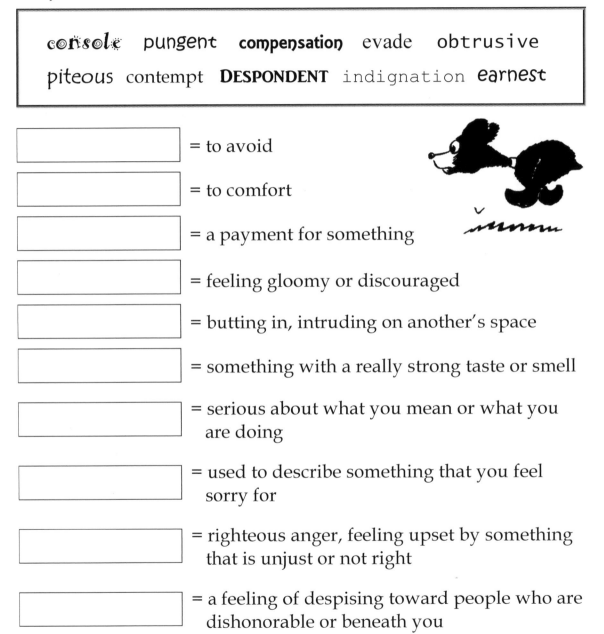

	= to avoid
	= to comfort
	= a payment for something
	= feeling gloomy or discouraged
	= butting in, intruding on another's space
	= something with a really strong taste or smell
	= serious about what you mean or what you are doing
	= used to describe something that you feel sorry for
	= righteous anger, feeling upset by something that is unjust or not right
	= a feeling of despising toward people who are dishonorable or beneath you

Heidi II Spelling

something with a really strong taste or smell

P	U			N	

to comfort

C		S		E

a feeling of despising toward people who are dishonorable

C		T			T

butting in, intruding on another's space

O			S	V	

feeling gloomy or discouraged

D		P		D		

righteous anger, feeling upset by something that is unjust or not right

I		D		G		T			

a payment for something

C		M	P				T			

Heidi II Crossword

Across

1. a payment for something
3. feeling gloomy or discouraged
7. used to describe something that you feel sorry for
8. something with a really strong taste or smell

Down

2. to avoid
4. to comfort
5. butting in, intruding on another's space
6. serious about what you mean or what you are doing

Heidi II Word Search

Find the hidden words and explain their meanings. The words can go in any direction, even backwards! The solution is on page 72.

L	R	N	N	M	P	C	I	S	S
B	E	U	O	W	V	O	N	U	O
W	Z	N	I	L	E	N	D	O	K
A	S	J	T	D	P	S	I	E	X
T	E	O	A	Y	E	O	G	T	H
A	T	V	S	V	V	L	N	I	Z
X	E	S	N	G	I	E	A	P	E
I	Z	T	E	N	S	R	T	V	S
J	G	C	P	N	U	G	I	D	G
K	N	A	M	R	R	F	O	E	A
C	B	U	O	D	T	A	N	Z	T
U	A	D	C	H	B	L	E	N	J
T	N	E	D	N	O	P	S	E	D
C	O	N	T	E	M	P	T	M	H
T	N	E	G	N	U	P	X	N	G

evade

earnest

pungent

console

piteous

obtrusive

contempt

despondent

indignation

compensation

"I want to
go about like the
light-footed goats."
– Johanna Spyri

Heidi II Fill-in-the-Blanks

Fill in the blanks to complete the sentences. Change the word forms if necessary.

piteous	CONSOLE	contempt	compensation	evade
obtrusive	despondent	earnest	indignation	pungent

1. It was a _____ sight to see.

2. He is _____ in his endeavors.

3. She looked at him with _____.

4. The taste is similar, but not as _____.

5. She earns a lot of _____ for her work.

6. You always laugh and _____ the question.

7. When I was robbed, I was filled with _____.

8. Nothing could _____ him when his wife died.

9. It's difficult to work with a loud, _____ person.

10. My little brother was _____ after losing the game.

Heidi III Vocabulary

Review and read aloud the words and their meanings.

indignant = feeling upset over something that is not right

retort = to answer back in an angry way

intimidate = to fill someone with fear

accost = to confront boldly

infirm = weak, sickly, frail

atrocious = shockingly bad

perplexity = confusion

obstinate = stubborn

vivacity = liveliness

fret = to worry

✓ Don't <u>fret</u> if we're a few minutes late.
✓ "Don't be ridiculous!" he <u>retorted</u> angrily.
✓ My grandfather became <u>infirm</u> with old age.
✓ He refused to be <u>intimidated</u> by their threats.
✓ Most of them just stared at her in <u>perplexity</u>.
✓ He can be very <u>obstinate</u> when he wants to be!
✓ I was charmed by her <u>vivacity</u> and high spirits.
✓ She was <u>accosted</u> in the street by a complete stranger.
✓ She was very <u>indignant</u> at the way she had been treated.
✓ The storm was <u>atrocious</u>, with heavy rain and hailstones.

Heidi III Matching

Can you match the words with their definitions?

indignant   vivacity

obstinate   accost

intimidate   **fret**

INFIRM   retort

perplexity   **ATROCIOUS**

	= to worry
	= liveliness
	= stubborn
	= confusion
	= weak, sickly, frail
	= to confront boldly
	= shockingly bad
	= to fill someone with fear
	= to answer back in an angry way
	= feeling upset over something that is not right

28

Heidi III Spelling

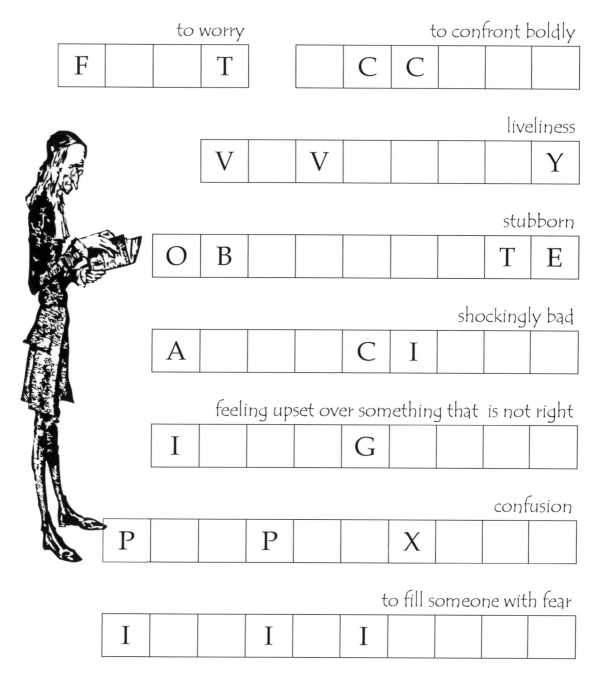

to worry

F			T

to confront boldly

	C	C		

liveliness

V		V				Y

stubborn

O	B					T	E

shockingly bad

A			C	I			

feeling upset over something that is not right

I			G			

confusion

P		P		X		

to fill someone with fear

I		I		I			

Heidi III Word Pieces

Use the pieces below to build words with the given definitions.

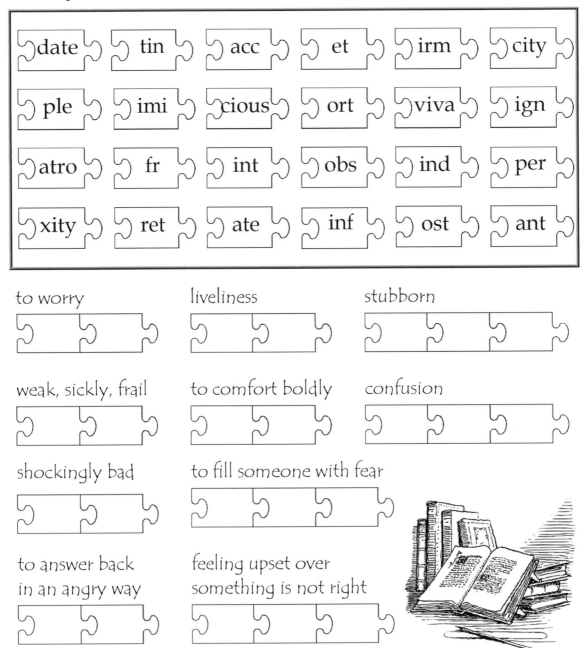

date	tin	acc	et	irm	city
ple	imi	cious	ort	viva	ign
atro	fr	int	obs	ind	per
xity	ret	ate	inf	ost	ant

to worry

liveliness

stubborn

weak, sickly, frail

to comfort boldly

confusion

shockingly bad

to fill someone with fear

to answer back
in an angry way

feeling upset over
something is not right

Heidi III Word Jumble

Unscramble the jumbled words.

stubborn

S E T N T I A O B   → _____

to fill someone with fear

I N A E I M D I T T   → _____

to worry

R T E F   → _____

confusion

P R L Y P T E I E X   → _____

liveliness

A I Y I V V T C   → _____

shockingly bad

C O O S R U I T A   → _____

to confront boldly

T C O S A C   → _____

weak, sickly, frail

F I R N I M   → _____

Heidi III Fill-in-the-Blanks

Fill in the blanks to complete the sentences. Change the word forms if necessary.

atrocious	OBSTINATE	fret	intimidate	accost
retort	perplexity	indignant	infirm	vivacity

1. Don't _____ if we're a few minutes late.

2. "Don't be ridiculous!" he _____ angrily.

3. My grandfather became _____ with old age.

4. He refused to be _____ by their threats.

5. Most of them just stared at her in _____.

6. He can be very _____ when he wants to be!

7. I was charmed by her _____ and high spirits.

8. She was _____ in the street by a complete stranger.

9. The storm was _____, with heavy rain and hailstones.

10. She was very _____ at the way she had been treated.

Five Little Peppers Vocabulary

Review and read aloud the words and their meanings.

disdainfully =	with contempt, scornfully, to look down on others or something
eminent =	prominent, noteworthy, and important
dismally =	with gloom and dreariness, pitifully
deliberation =	carefully thinking over a decision
ample =	full, enough, plentiful
incredulously =	with unbelief
obliged =	required
anxiety =	worry

- ✓ After ten hours of <u>deliberation</u>, the jury returned a verdict of 'not guilty'.
- ✓ I tried hard but failed <u>dismally</u>.
- ✓ There is <u>ample</u> pizza for all of us.
- ✓ She is <u>eminent</u> in the field of mathematics.
- ✓ She replied <u>incredulously</u>, "I don't believe it!"
- ✓ The judge looked <u>disdainfully</u> at the criminal.
- ✓ During thunderstorms, dogs may experience <u>anxiety</u>.
- ✓ Mr. Sesemann now beckoned to the children as it was time to be off. Grandmamma's white horse had been brought up for Clara, as she was no longer <u>obliged</u> to be carried in a chair. – *Heidi*

Five Little Peppers Matching

Can you match the words with their definitions?

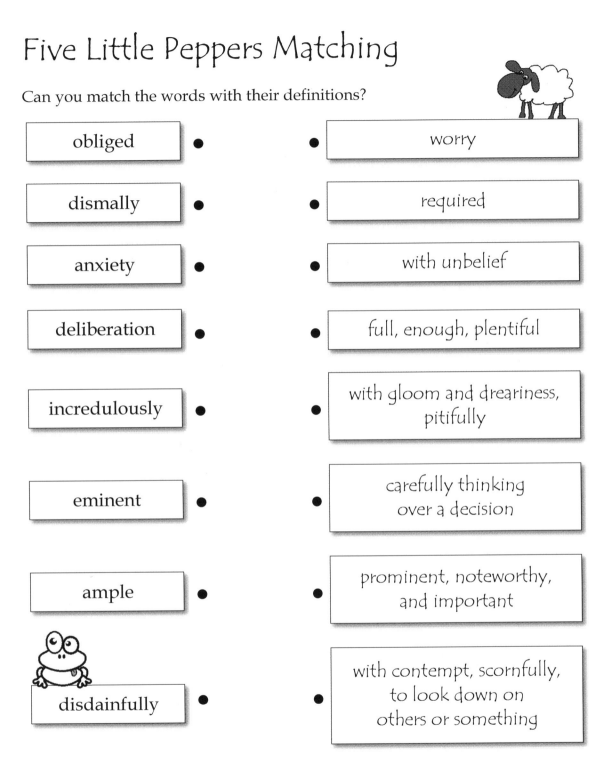

obliged	worry
dismally	required
anxiety	with unbelief
deliberation	full, enough, plentiful
incredulously	with gloom and dreariness, pitifully
eminent	carefully thinking over a decision
ample	prominent, noteworthy, and important
disdainfully	with contempt, scornfully, to look down on others or something

Five Little Peppers Spelling

with contempt, scornfully, to look down on others or something

D			D		N				Y

carefully thinking over a decision

D			B			T		

with gloom and dreariness, pitifully

D		M		L	

prominent, noteworthy, and important

E		N		

worry

A	X	E	

required

O	B				

full, enough, plentiful

	M		E

Five Little Peppers Crossword

Across
3. with unbelief
6. full, enough, plentiful
7. with gloom and dreariness, pitifully
8. with contempt, scornfully, to look down on others or something

Down
1. worry   2. required
4. carefully thinking over decision
5. prominent, noteworthy, and important

Five Little Peppers Word Jumble

Unscramble these jumbles to find a hidden word.

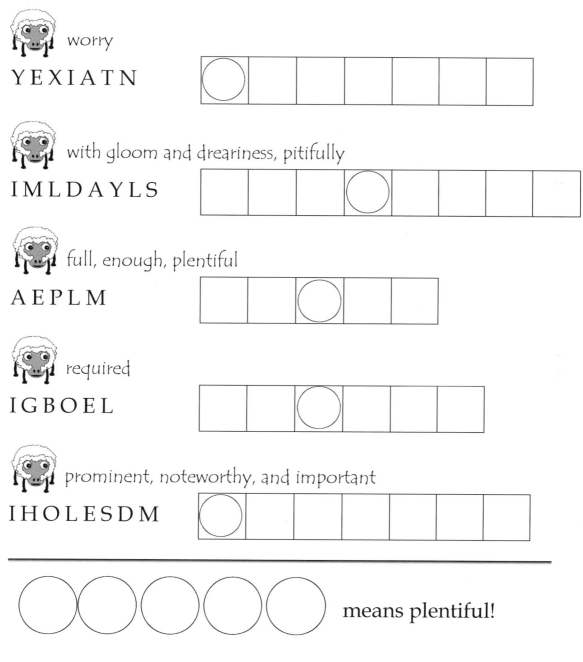

worry

Y E X I A T N

with gloom and dreariness, pitifully

I M L D A Y L S

full, enough, plentiful

A E P L M

required

I G B O E L

prominent, noteworthy, and important

I H O L E S D M

means plentiful!

Five Little Peppers Fill-in-the-Blanks

Fill in the blanks to complete the sentences. Change the word forms if necessary.

incredulously   AMPLE   **disdainfully**   DISMALLY

obliged   eminent   deliberation   **anxiety**

1. I tried hard but failed _____.

2. There is _____ pizza for all of us.

3. She replied _____, "I don't believe it!"

4. The judge looked _____ at the criminal.

5. She is _____ in the field of mathematics.

6. During thunderstorms, dogs may experience _____.

7. After ten hours of _____, the jury returned a verdict of 'not guilty'.

8. Mr. Sesemann now beckoned to the children as it was time to be off. Grandmamma's white horse had been brought up for Clara, as she was no longer _____ to be carried in a chair. – *Heidi*

Vocabulary Review Matching I

Can you match the words with their definitions?

Vexed	pungent	quarrel	NECESSITY
obtrusive	loiter	deliberation	acquaintance
imposing	indignant	dismally	disdainfully

_____ = to have an argument

_____ = frustrated and annoyed

_____ = something that is needed

_____ = grand and impressive in appearance

_____ = a person you know but not very well

_____ = butting in, intruding on another's space

_____ = something with a really strong taste or smell

_____ = feeling upset over something that is not right

_____ = carefully thinking over a decision

_____ = with gloom and dreariness, pitifully

_____ = with contempt, scornfully, to look down on others or something

_____ = to dawdle over your work or to hang around some place without any purpose

Vocabulary Review Matching II

Can you match the words with their definitions?

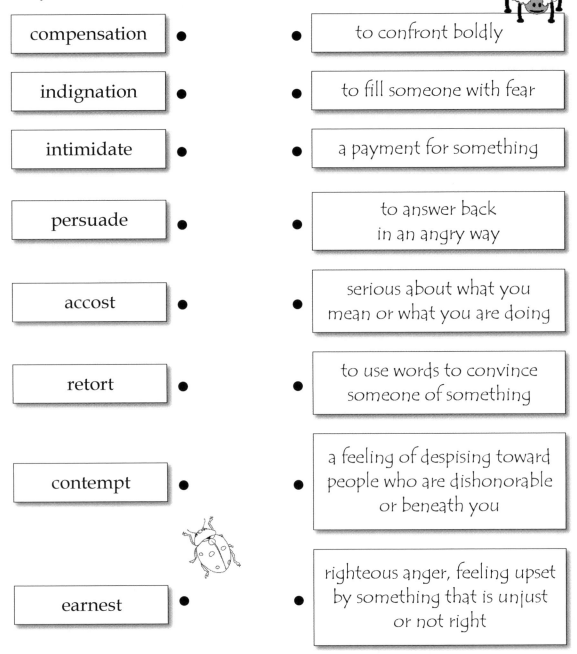

compensation	•	•	to confront boldly
indignation	•	•	to fill someone with fear
intimidate	•	•	a payment for something
persuade	•	•	to answer back in an angry way
accost	•	•	serious about what you mean or what you are doing
retort	•	•	to use words to convince someone of something
contempt	•	•	a feeling of despising toward people who are dishonorable or beneath you
earnest	•	•	righteous anger, feeling upset by something that is unjust or not right

Vocabulary Review Matching III

Can you match the words with their definitions?

evade   DESPONDENT   scold

fierce   atROCIOUS   ample

eminent   fret

vigorous   luscious   piteous

Heidi learns to
make doll clothes

	= reproach
	= to worry
	= to avoid
	= shockingly bad
	= strong and active
	= ferocious, wild, and violent
	= full, enough, plentiful
	= highly pleasing to the senses
	= feeling gloomy or discouraged
	= prominent, noteworthy, and important
	= used to describe something that you feel sorry for

41

Vocabulary Review Matching IV

Can you match the words with their definitions?

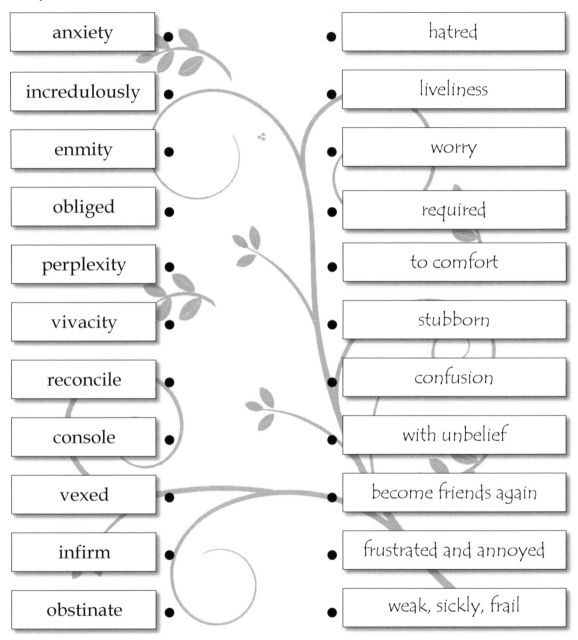

anxiety	hatred
incredulously	liveliness
enmity	worry
obliged	required
perplexity	to comfort
vivacity	stubborn
reconcile	confusion
console	with unbelief
vexed	become friends again
infirm	frustrated and annoyed
obstinate	weak, sickly, frail

Vocabulary Review Crossword I

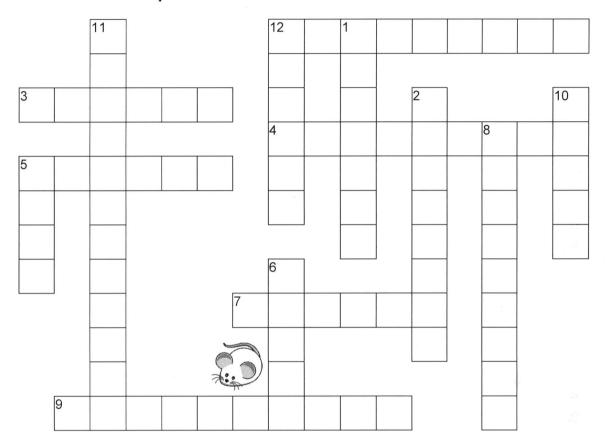

Across

3. hatred
4. stubborn
5. ferocious, wild and violent
7. to confront boldly
9. to fill someone with fear
12. become friends again

Down

1. to comfort
2. liveliness
8. shockingly bad
10. frustrated and annoyed
11. a payment for something
12. to answer back in an angry way

5. to worry
6. reproach

Vocabulary Review Crossword II

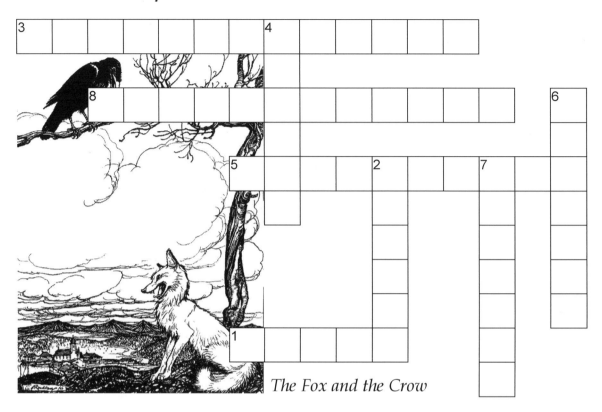

The Fox and the Crow

Across

1. to avoid   3. with unbelief

5. feeling gloomy or discouraged

8. with contempt, scornfully,

to look down on others or something

Down

2. required

4. to hang around some place without any purpose

6. used to describe something that you feel sorry for

7. serious about what you mean or what you are doing

44

Vocabulary Review Crossword III

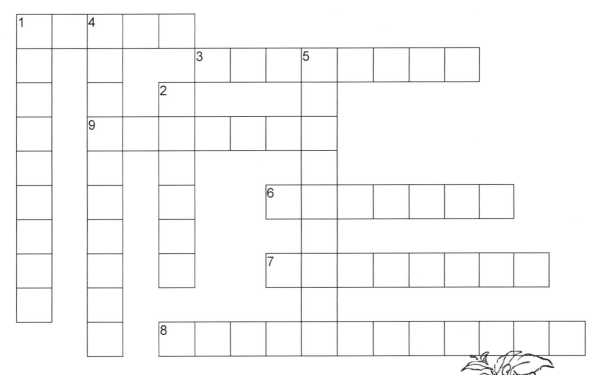

Across

1. full, enough, plentiful
3. strong and active
6. to have an argument
7. with gloom and dreariness, pitifully
8. acting like someone else is beneath you
9. something with a really strong taste or smell

Down

1. shockingly bad   2. hatred   4. confusion
5. butting in, intruding on another's space

Vocabulary Review Word Search I

Find the hidden words and explain their meanings. The words can go in any direction, even backwards! The solution is on page 73.

B	P	A	I	N	F	I	R	M	T	A	D	E	V
I	E	N	J	T	Y	H	G	P	U	Q	N	V	I
E	L	X	F	O	N	X	M	E	G	M	A	I	G
N	O	I	T	A	R	E	B	I	L	E	D	S	O
M	S	E	D	I	T	E	D	R	D	L	E	U	R
I	N	T	L	N	M	S	M	N	E	R	C	R	O
T	O	Y	O	M	S	P	U	I	O	T	S	T	U
Y	C	C	C	T	B	D	O	O	N	P	I	B	S
P	E	R	S	U	A	D	E	S	E	E	S	O	V
S	U	O	I	C	S	U	L	X	I	T	N	E	L
O	B	L	I	G	E	D	A	V	E	N	I	T	D
A	N	W	E	E	C	R	E	I	F	V	G	P	K

despondent   vigorous   infirm   persuade   scold

imposing   eminent   loiter   piteous   fierce

contempt   enmity   obliged   anxiety   evade

deliberation   obtrusive   luscious   console   vexed

46

Vocabulary Review Word Search II

Find the hidden words and explain their meanings. The words can go in any direction, even backwards! The solution is on page 74.

Y	A	O	A	N	P	S	N	P	N
L	C	B	X	O	E	U	E	D	O
S	Q	S	K	I	R	O	C	I	I
U	U	T	E	T	P	I	E	S	T
O	A	I	L	A	L	C	S	D	A
L	I	N	I	S	E	O	S	A	N
U	N	A	C	N	X	R	I	I	G
D	T	T	N	E	I	T	T	N	I
E	A	E	O	P	T	A	Y	F	D
R	N	R	C	M	Y	B	Q	U	N
C	C	F	E	O	W	X	G	L	I
N	E	D	R	C	A	M	P	L	E
I	V	I	V	A	C	I	T	Y	S
T	N	T	I	M	I	D	A	T	E
T	N	A	N	G	I	D	N	I	Z

fret

ample

vivacity

indignant

atrocious

necessity

reconcile

obstinate

intimidate

perplexity

indignation

disdainfully

incredulously

acquaintance

compensation

47

Vocabulary Review Word Jumble I

Unscramble these jumbles to find a hidden word.

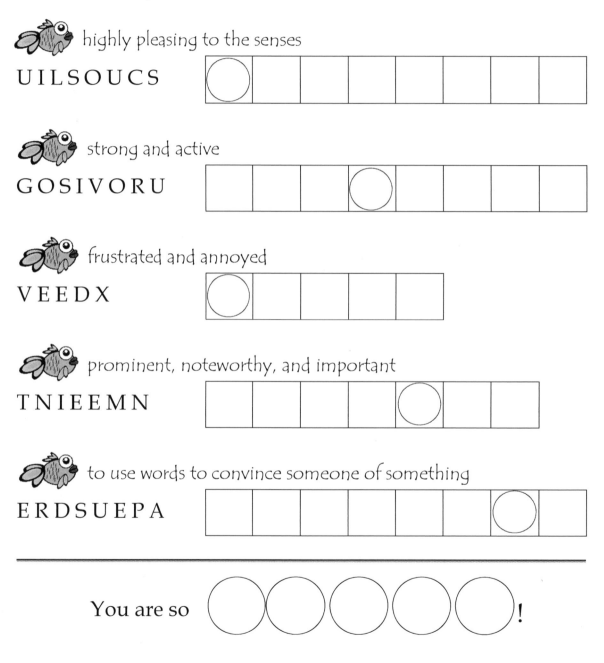

highly pleasing to the senses

UILSOUCS

strong and active

GOSIVORU

frustrated and annoyed

VEEDX

prominent, noteworthy, and important

TNIEEMN

to use words to convince someone of something

ERDSUEPA

You are so ⚪⚪⚪⚪⚪!

Vocabulary Review Word Jumble II

Unscramble these jumbles to find a hidden word.

ferocious, wild and violent

IFRCEE

full, enough, plentiful

EAPLM

required

OEBIGL

reproach

SCDLO

to comfort

NOCSOEL

I love reading ⭕⭕⭕⭕⭕ s!

Vocabulary Review Word Jumble III

Unscramble the jumbled words.

a feeling of despising toward people who are dishonorable

CTNETMPO → _____

a payment for something

OIEMOPTNSANC → _____

a person you know but not very well

NANCIUAQCAET → _____

becoming friends again

ECNIOLECR → _____

butting in, intruding on another's space

TRIUOEVBS → _____

carefully thinking over a decision

DTELANRIIOEB → _____

confusion

TEEPRPIXLY → _____

feeling gloomy or discouraged

PENSTEODDN → _____

Vocabulary Review Word Jumble **IV**

Unscramble the jumbled words.

feeling upset over something that is not right

A N N D G I T N I   → _____

grand and impressive in appearance

M I I S O P G N   → _____

hatred

M T Y E N I   → _____

liveliness

T A C V I Y I V   → _____

righteous anger, feeling upset by something that is unjust

T N I O G I N N A I D   → _____

serious about what you mean or what you are doing

T E R E S A N   → _____

shockingly bad

T O S I O C A R U   → _____

something that is needed

E S C I E S T N Y   → _____

Vocabulary Review Word Jumble V

Unscramble the jumbled words.

something with a really strong taste or smell

PNUENTG → _____

stubborn

TSIBEAOTN → _____

to answer back in an angry way

OTERTR → _____

to avoid

DEEVA → _____

to confront boldly

TAOCCS → _____

to fill someone with fear

AIMTNITIED → _____

to have an argument

URQELRA → _____

to worry

FETR → _____

Vocabulary Review Word Jumble VI

Unscramble the jumbled words.

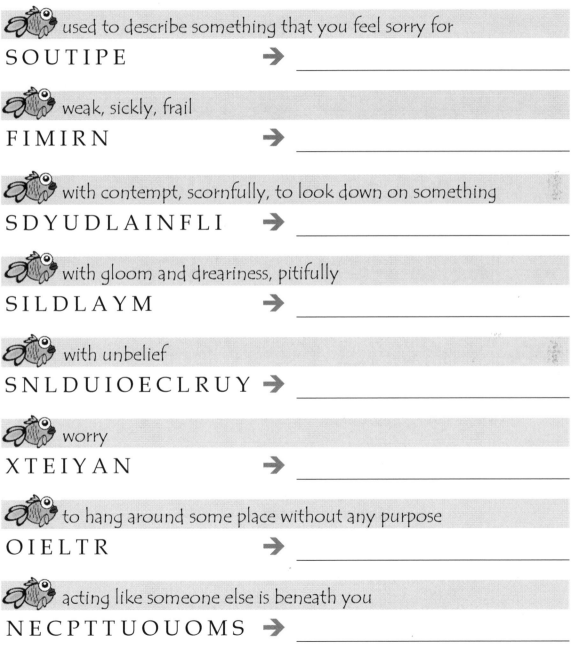

used to describe something that you feel sorry for

S O U T I P E ➔ _____

weak, sickly, frail

F I M I R N ➔ _____

with contempt, scornfully, to look down on something

S D Y U D L A I N F L I ➔ _____

with gloom and dreariness, pitifully

S I L D L A Y M ➔ _____

with unbelief

S N L D U I O E C L R U Y ➔ _____

worry

X T E I Y A N ➔ _____

to hang around some place without any purpose

O I E L T R ➔ _____

acting like someone else is beneath you

N E C P T T U O U O M S ➔ _____

Vocabulary Review Fill-in-the-Blanks I

Fill in the blanks to complete the sentences. Change the word forms if necessary.

obstinate	compensation	dismally	ANXIETY
obtrusive	infirm	enmity	intimidate
despondent	pungent	vexed	ample

1. I'm rather _____ with him. He never puts the tools away.

2. During thunderstorms, dogs may experience _____.

3. My little brother was _____ after losing the game.

4. They fight because there is _____ between them.

5. It's difficult to work with a loud, _____ person.

6. My grandfather became _____ with old age.

7. He can be very _____ when he wants to be!

8. He refused to be _____ by their threats.

9. The taste is similar, but not as _____.

10. She earns a lot of _____ for her work.

11. I tried hard but failed _____.

12. There is _____ pizza for all of us.

Vocabulary Review Fill-in-the-Blanks II

Fill in the blanks to complete the sentences. Change the word forms if necessary.

deliberation	earnest	vivacity	LUSCIOUS
loiter	eminent	accost	acquaintance
necessity	imposing	retort	contempt

1. He is _____ in his endeavors.

2. She looked at him with _____.

3. _____ is the mother of invention.

4. He is not a friend, only an _____.

5. The herb garden is full of _____ herbs.

6. "Don't be ridiculous!" he _____ angrily.

7. She is _____ in the field of mathematics.

8. An _____ house towers high over the hill.

9. I was charmed by her _____ and high spirits.

10. Teenagers were _____ in the street outside.

11. She was _____ in the street by a complete stranger.

12. After ten hours of _____, the jury returned a verdict of 'not guilty'.

Vocabulary Review Fill-in-the-Blanks III

Fill in the blanks to complete the sentences. Change the word forms if necessary.

incredulously	perplexity	evade	SCOLD
DISDAINFULLY	piteous	atrocious	vigorous
indignation	indignant	console	fret

1. It was a _____ sight to see.

2. She replied _____, "I don't believe it!"

3. Don't _____ if we're a few minutes late.

4. The judge looked _____ at the criminal.

5. You always laugh and _____ the question.

6. Most of them just stared at her in _____.

7. When I was robbed, I was filled with _____.

8. The United States is a young, _____ country.

9. Nothing could _____ him when his wife died.

10. She was very _____ at the way she had been treated.

11. The storm was _____, with heavy rain and hailstones.

12. If you _____ your child too much, he will lose confidence.

Synonyms Matching I

Synonyms are words that have the same or nearly the same meaning. Connect the words with their synonyms. The solution is on page 75.

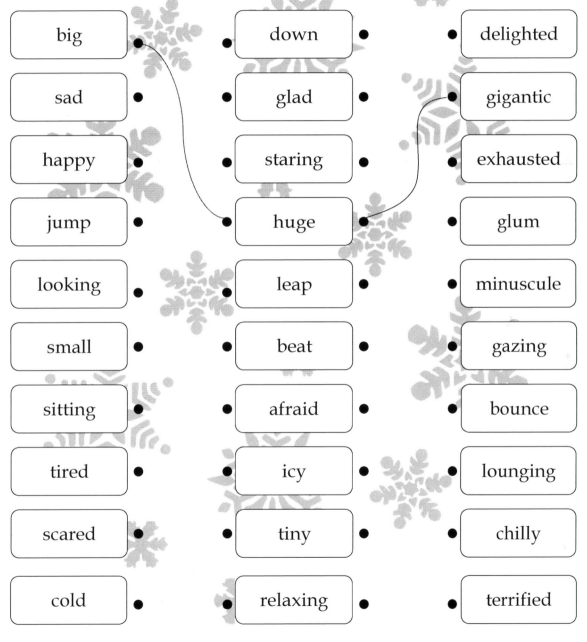

big	down	delighted
sad	glad	gigantic
happy	staring	exhausted
jump	huge	glum
looking	leap	minuscule
small	beat	gazing
sitting	afraid	bounce
tired	icy	lounging
scared	tiny	chilly
cold	relaxing	terrified

Synonyms Matching II

Synonyms are words that have the same or nearly the same meaning. Can you match the words with their synonyms? The solution is on page 75.

solution	●	●	garbage
ruin	●	●	chair
gaze	●	●	answer
rescue	●	●	funny
giggle	●	●	save
extend	●	●	woods
trash	●	●	look
silly	●	●	destroy
seat	●	●	stretch
forest	●	●	laugh

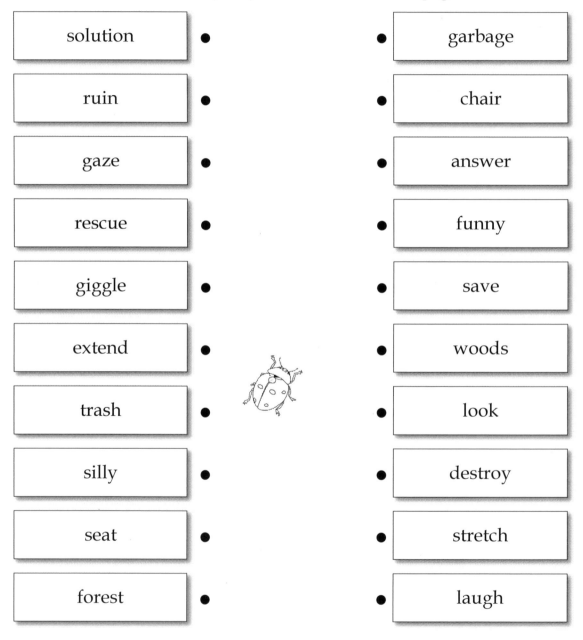

Synonyms Matching III

Synonyms are words that have the same or nearly the same meaning. Can you match the words with their synonyms? The solution is on page 75.

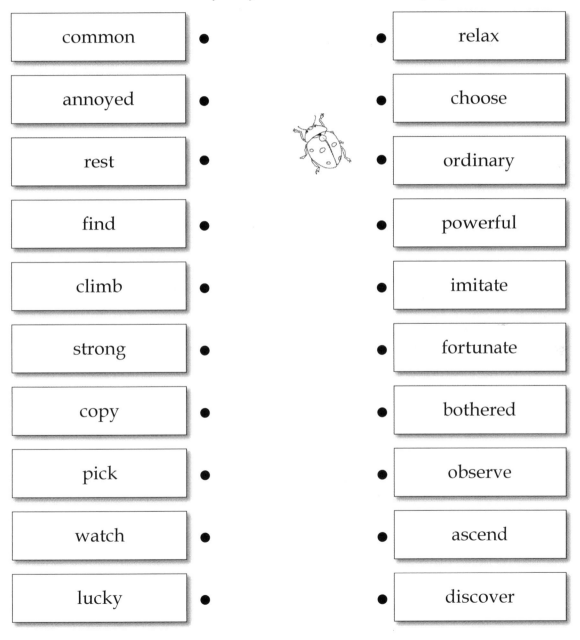

common ●	● relax
annoyed ●	● choose
rest ●	● ordinary
find ●	● powerful
climb ●	● imitate
strong ●	● fortunate
copy ●	● bothered
pick ●	● observe
watch ●	● ascend
lucky ●	● discover

Synonyms Matching IV

The Ox and the Frog

Synonyms are words that have the same or nearly the same meaning. Can you match the words with their synonyms? The solution is on page 76.

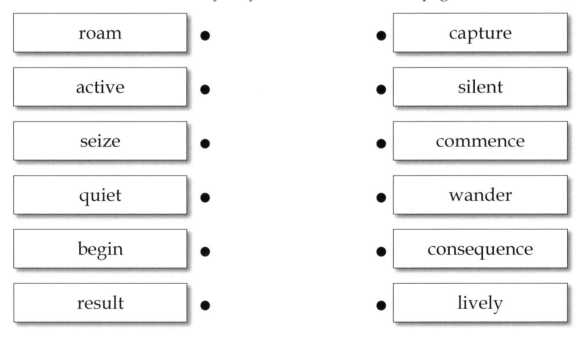

roam	•	•	capture
active	•	•	silent
seize	•	•	commence
quiet	•	•	wander
begin	•	•	consequence
result	•	•	lively

Synonyms Matching V

Synonyms are words that have the same or nearly the same meaning. Write a synonym for each word. Use the words from the word box. The solution is on page 76.

Happy mad trousers clad BRIEF ask envy

smart land job DROWSY Hazard BUILD ALIKE

conflict Lead achieve dismay loud Crafty

noisy			sneaky	
construct			ground	
concise			same	
jealousy			fight	
covered			guide	
angry			sleepy	
pants			clever	
inquire			accomplish	
rapturous			occupation	
danger			distress	

Antonyms Matching I

Antonyms are words that have opposite or nearly opposite meanings. Can you match the words with their antonyms? The solution is on page 77.

future	shorten
lengthen	descend
natural	fade
lazy	separate
brighten	past
combine	reveal
blame	artificial
ascend	tireless
conceal	abundant
rare	praise

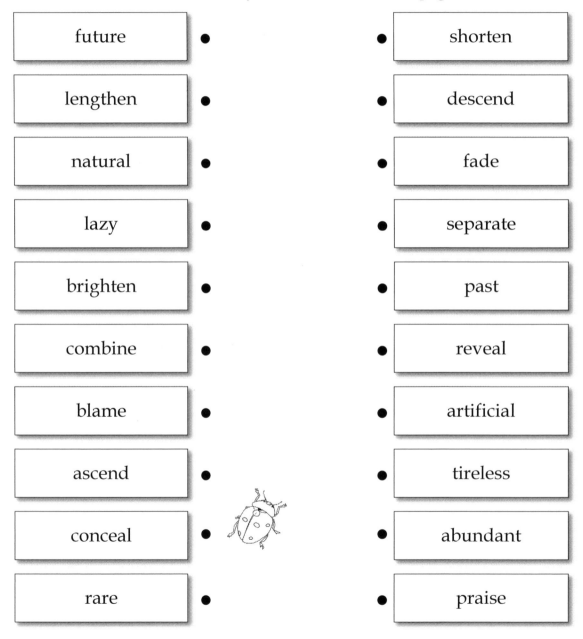

Antonyms Matching II

Antonyms are words that have opposite or nearly opposite meanings. Can you match the words with their antonyms? The solution is on page 77.

increase	hindering
export	dead
helpful	fail
dusk	foolish
alive	shallow
succeed	import
feeble	decrease
deep	sour
wise	dawn
sweet	strong

Antonyms Matching III

Antonyms are words that have opposite or nearly opposite meanings. Can you match the words with their antonyms? The solution is on page 77.

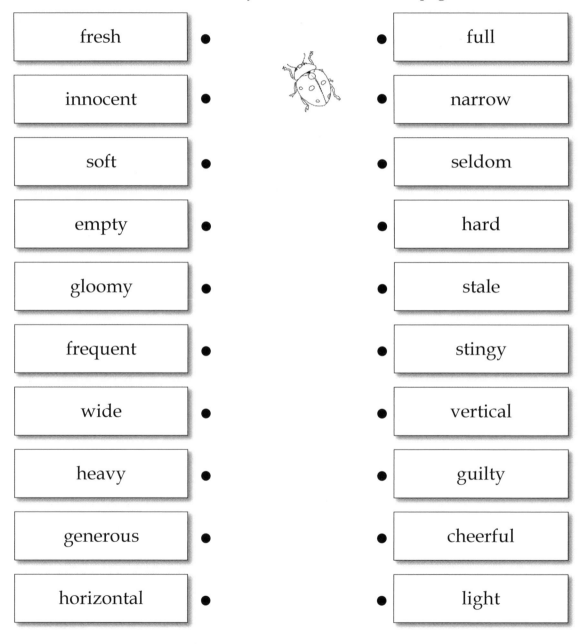

fresh	full
innocent	narrow
soft	seldom
empty	hard
gloomy	stale
frequent	stingy
wide	vertical
heavy	guilty
generous	cheerful
horizontal	light

Antonyms Matching IV

The Fox and the Lion

Antonyms are words that have opposite or nearly opposite meanings. Can you match the words with their antonyms? The solution is on page 77.

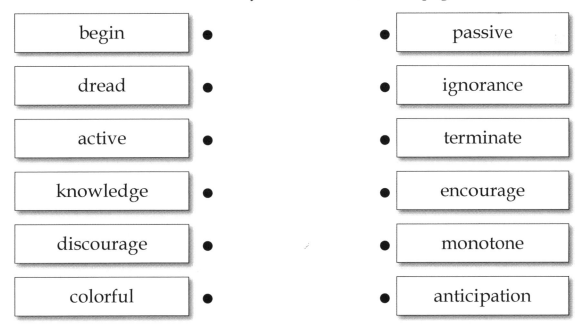

begin ●	● passive
dread ●	● ignorance
active ●	● terminate
knowledge ●	● encourage
discourage ●	● monotone
colorful ●	● anticipation

Antonyms Crossword

Antonyms are words that have opposite or nearly opposite meanings. The solution is on page 78.

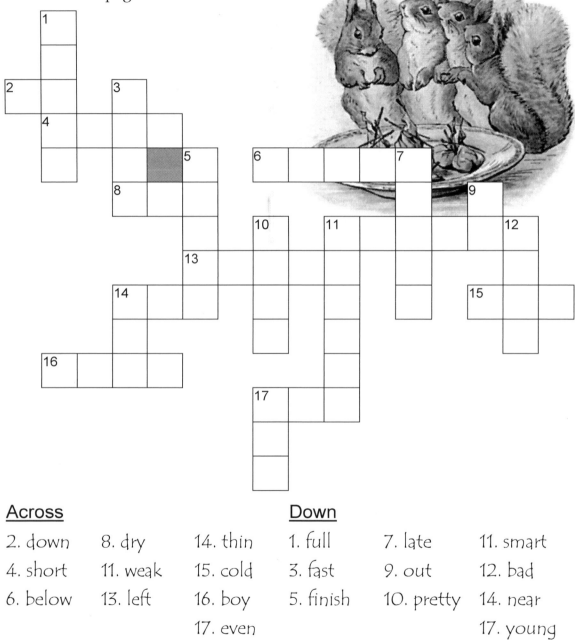

Across

2. down	8. dry	14. thin
4. short	11. weak	15. cold
6. below	13. left	16. boy
		17. even

Down

1. full	7. late	11. smart
3. fast	9. out	12. bad
5. finish	10. pretty	14. near
		17. young

U.S. States Map Trivia I

Match the names of states with their abbreviations.

		Missouri	Pennsylvania
Alabama	Illinois	Montana	Rhode Island
Alaska	Indiana	Nebraska	South Carolina
Arizona	Iowa	Nevada	South Dakota
Arkansas	Kansas	New Hampshire	Tennessee
California	Kentucky	New Jersey	Texas
Colorado	Louisiana	New Mexico	Utah
Connecticut	Maine	New York	Vermont
Delaware	Maryland	North Carolina	Virginia
Florida	Massachusetts	North Dakota	Washington
Georgia	Michigan	Ohio	West Virginia
Hawaii	Minnesota	Oklahoma	Wisconsin
Idaho	Mississippi	Oregon	Wyoming

U.S. States Map Trivia II

Can you identify the states on the map?

		Missouri	Pennsylvania
Alabama	Illinois	Montana	Rhode Island
Alaska	Indiana	Nebraska	South Carolina
Arizona	Iowa	Nevada	South Dakota
Arkansas	Kansas	New Hampshire	Tennessee
California	Kentucky	New Jersey	Texas
Colorado	Louisiana	New Mexico	Utah
Connecticut	Maine	New York	Vermont
Delaware	Maryland	North Carolina	Virginia
Florida	Massachusetts	North Dakota	Washington
Georgia	Michigan	Ohio	West Virginia
Hawaii	Minnesota	Oklahoma	Wisconsin
Idaho	Mississippi	Oregon	Wyoming

U.S. States Fill-In Crossword

Fill in the names of states. The solution is on page 79.

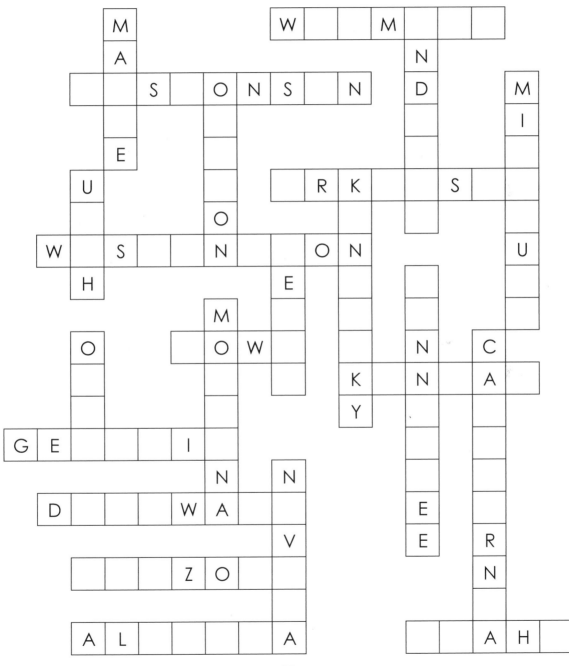

Solutions to Selected Puzzles

HEIDI I WORD SEARCH

The first letters are marked. Remember that the words can go in any direction, even backwards!

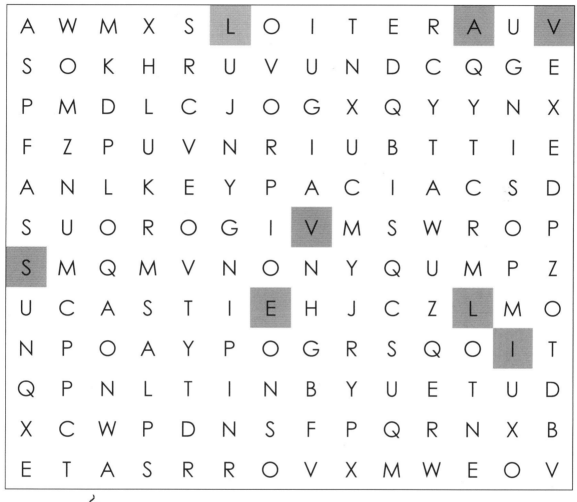

A	W	M	X	S	L	O	I	T	E	R	A	U	V
S	O	K	H	R	U	V	U	N	D	C	Q	G	E
P	M	D	L	C	J	O	G	X	Q	Y	Y	N	X
F	Z	P	U	V	N	R	I	U	B	T	T	I	E
A	N	L	K	E	Y	P	A	C	I	A	C	S	D
S	U	O	R	O	G	I	V	M	S	W	R	O	P
S	M	Q	M	V	N	O	N	Y	Q	U	M	P	Z
U	C	A	S	T	I	E	H	J	C	Z	L	M	O
N	P	O	A	Y	P	O	G	R	S	Q	O	I	T
Q	P	N	L	T	I	N	B	Y	U	E	T	U	D
X	C	W	P	D	N	S	F	P	Q	R	N	X	B
E	T	A	S	R	R	O	V	X	M	W	E	O	V

enmity   luscious

loiter   vigorous

imposing   vexed

acquaintance   scold

71

HEIDI II WORD SEARCH

The first letters are marked. Remember that the words can go in any direction, even backwards!

L	R	N	N	M	P	C	I	S	S
B	E	U	O	W	V	O	N	U	O
W	Z	N	I	L	E	N	D	O	K
A	S	J	T	D	P	S	I	E	X
T	E	O	A	Y	E	O	G	T	H
A	T	V	S	V	V	L	N	I	Z
X	E	S	N	G	I	E	A	P	E
I	Z	T	E	N	S	R	T	V	S
J	G	C	P	N	U	G	I	D	G
K	N	A	M	R	R	F	O	E	A
C	B	U	O	D	T	A	N	Z	T
U	A	D	C	H	B	L	E	N	J
T	N	E	D	N	O	P	S	E	D
C	O	N	T	E	M	P	T	M	H
T	N	E	G	N	U	P	X	N	G

evade

earnest

pungent

console

piteous

obtrusive

contempt

despondent

indignation

compensation

"I want to go about like the light-footed goats."
– Johanna Spyri

72

VOCABULARY REVIEW WORD SEARCH I

The first letters are marked. Remember that the words can go in any direction, even backwards!

B	P	A	I	N	F	I	R	M	T	A	D	E	V
I	E	N	J	T	Y	H	G	P	U	Q	N	V	I
E	L	X	F	O	N	X	M	E	G	M	A	I	G
N	O	I	T	A	R	E	B	I	L	E	D	S	O
M	S	E	D	I	T	E	D	R	D	L	E	U	R
I	N	T	L	N	M	S	M	N	E	R	C	R	O
T	O	Y	O	M	S	P	U	I	O	T	S	T	U
Y	C	C	C	T	B	D	O	O	N	P	I	B	S
P	E	R	S	U	A	D	E	S	E	E	S	O	V
S	U	O	I	C	S	U	L	X	I	T	N	E	L
O	B	L	I	G	E	D	A	V	E	N	I	T	D
A	N	W	E	E	C	R	E	I	F	V	G	P	K

despondent	vigorous	infirm	persuade	scold
imposing	eminent	loiter	piteous	fierce
contempt	enmity	obliged	anxiety	evade
deliberation	obtrusive	luscious	console	vexed

VOCABULARY REVIEW WORD SEARCH II

The first letters are marked. Remember that the words can go in any direction, even backwards!

Y	A	O	A	N	P	S	N	P	N
L	C	B	X	O	E	U	E	D	O
S	Q	S	K	I	R	O	C	I	I
U	U	T	E	T	P	I	E	S	T
O	A	I	L	A	L	C	S	D	A
L	I	N	I	S	E	O	S	A	N
U	N	A	C	N	X	R	I	I	G
D	T	T	N	E	I	T	T	N	I
E	A	E	O	P	T	A	Y	F	D
R	N	R	C	M	Y	B	Q	U	N
C	C	F	E	O	W	X	G	L	I
N	E	D	R	C	A	M	P	L	E
I	V	I	V	A	C	I	T	Y	S
T	N	T	I	M	I	D	A	T	E
T	N	A	N	G	I	D	N	I	Z

fret

ample

vivacity

indignant

atrocious

necessity

reconcile

obstinate

intimidate

perplexity

indignation

disdainfully

incredulously

acquaintance

compensation

74

SYNONYMS MATCHING I, II, & III

big – huge – gigantic	small – tiny – minuscule
sad – down – glum	sitting – relaxing – lounging
happy – glad – delighted	tired – beat – exhausted
jump – leap – bounce	scared – afraid – terrified
looking – staring – gazing	cold – icy – chilly

solution – answer	extend – stretch
ruin – destroy	trash – garbage
gaze – look	silly – funny
rescue – save	seat – chair
giggle – laugh	forest – woods

common – ordinary	strong – powerful
annoyed – bothered	copy – imitate
rest – relax	pick – choose
find – discover	watch – observe
climb – ascend	lucky – fortunate

SYNONYMS MATCHING IV & V

roam – wander	quiet – silent
active – lively	begin – commence
seize – capture	result – consequence

noisy – loud	sneaky – crafty
construct – build	ground – land
concise – brief	same – alike
jealousy – envy	fight – conflict
covered – clad	guide – lead
angry – mad	sleepy – drowsy
pants – trousers	clever – smart
inquire – ask	accomplish – achieve
rapturous – happy	occupation – job
danger – hazard	distress – dismay

ANTONYMS MATCHING I, II, III & IV

future – past	combine – separate
lengthen – shorten	blame – praise
natural – artificial	ascend – descend
lazy – tireless	conceal – reveal
brighten – fade	rare – abundant

increase – decrease	succeed – fail
export – import	feeble – strong
helpful – hindering	deep – shallow
dusk – dawn	wise – foolish
alive – dead	sweet – sour

fresh – stale	frequent – seldom
innocent – guilty	wide – narrow
soft – hard	heavy – light
empty – full	generous – stingy
gloomy – cheerful	horizontal – vertical

begin – terminate	knowledge – ignorance
dread – anticipation	discourage – encourage
active – passive	colorful – monotone

ANTONYMS CROSSWORD

Across

2. down
4. short
6. below
8. dry
11. weak
13. left
14. thin
15. cold
16. boy
17. even

Down

1. full
3. fast
5. finish
7. late
9. out
10. pretty
11. smart
12. bad
14. near
17. young

U.S. STATES FILL-IN CROSSWORD

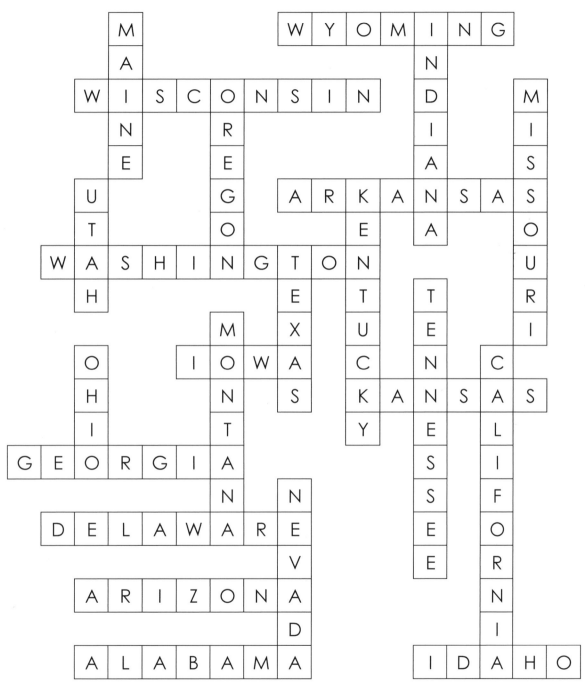

Made in the USA
Columbia, SC
11 October 2017